A DISCUSSION GUIDE ON
HISTORY'S MOST IMPORTANT EVENT

Experiencing THE PASSION of JESUS

LEE STROBEL / GARRY POOLE

ZONDERVAN™

GRAND RAPIDS, MICHIGAN 49530 USA

WILLOW
Willow Creek Resources

ZONDERVAN™

Experiencing the Passion of Jesus
Copyright © 2004 by Lee Strobel and Garry Poole

Requests for information should be addressed to:

Zondervan, *Grand Rapids, Michigan 49530*

ISBN: 0-7394-4379-8

Interior design by Todd Sprague

Printed in the United States of America

Contents

Preface

*I*n a darkened conference room at Mel Gibson's studio, the grisly execution of Jesus unfolded with jarring and vivid realism. Even though I was watching only a rough cut of the film *The Passion of the Christ,* it was as if I had a front-row seat to history!

For the first time in my life, I felt as if I were really *experiencing* what Jesus had endured. Book research, library studies, and interviews with scholars had given me cognitive knowledge, but now my heart engaged with history as never before. Tears flowed freely. The emotional impact of the film forever changed the way I would think about the crucifixion.

Flash back nearly a quarter of a century.

As a spiritual skeptic with an intellectual bent, I used to think the idea of God was absurd, that Jesus was merely a human being who was later mythologized into a god, and that death would completely extinguish my existence. I agreed with atheist Bertrand Russell: "I believe that when I die I shall rot, and nothing of my ego will survive."

Pretty grim—but hey, that's reality, I thought.

Then my wife became a Christian. Bad news, I figured. But in the ensuing months I became so intrigued by the positive changes in her character that I began to use my journalism and legal training to investigate whether there was any credibility to Christianity. For me, as legal editor of the *Chicago Tribune,* it was like pursuing the most important story of my life.

Much of my investigation focused on the passion (that is, the suffering and death) of Jesus of Nazareth and the related claims of his resurrection. It was important for me to establish whether he did, indeed, die on the cross before I could determine if there was sufficient reason to believe he was seen alive afterward.

So I plumbed the evidence through extensive research and interviews with experts. Over time I became knowledgeable about the facts surrounding Jesus' demise. I could recite the probable size of the nails pounded into his hands and feet. I could describe the wound to his side. I could detail his cause of death. I became a repository of information surrounding this gruesomely efficient form of execution the Romans had perfected.

Ultimately, after a wide-ranging investigation that spanned almost two years, I became convinced that Christ's death and resurrection authenticated his claim to being the unique Son of God. Compelled by the facts, I received him as my forgiver and leader.

Yet despite all of the data, details, and documentation I had committed to memory, it wasn't until I endured the visual intensity of Gibson's film that I was able to absorb the emotional impact of the passion of Jesus.

If you have seen the movie, you know how powerful it is. Perhaps the film not only bombarded your senses with the reality of the crucifixion, but it has also prompted a lot of questions. Even if you haven't seen the movie but have been caught up in the media buzz about it, maybe questions have stirred in your mind, such as:

- Who *really* killed Jesus?
- What crime did Jesus commit?
- Did it actually happen like that?
- Why did Jesus suffer and die?
- What did the resurrection accomplish?
- How is this story relevant to me?

Garry Poole and I produced this discussion guide to help you explore these issues with other seekers and Christians in a nonthreatening environment, where all viewpoints and observations are invited. Through this exciting and stimulating process, we hope you will discover solid answers that can form the basis for your ultimate decision about the relevance of Jesus to your life.

When I got the chance to talk to Gibson, I thanked him for making it impossible for me—or anyone else who sees his film—to ever gloss over the severity of Christ's sufferings again. As Dorothy Sayers said, "It's curious that people who are filled with horrified indignation whenever a cat kills a sparrow can hear the story of the killing of God told Sunday after Sunday and not experience any shock at all."

Gibson's film shocks its viewers. Whether it is because you've been stunned by his portrayal of Christ's passion or prompted by something else, you've picked up this guide to look for a way to make sense of this monumental event of history.

So engage, discuss, analyze, ponder, study, grapple, contemplate, debate, learn, deliberate, grow—and then decide for yourself. Meanwhile, throughout your journey, keep this in mind: *All of heaven is cheering you on!*

—Lee Strobel

Getting Started

Christianity maintains that God welcomes sincere examination and inquiry. In fact, it is a matter of historical record that Jesus encouraged such scrutiny. The Bible is not a secret kept only for the initiated few, but an open book, available for study and debate. The teachings of Christ are freely offered to all—the skeptic as well as the believer.

So here's an open invitation: Examine the claims, explore the options, and draw your own conclusions. In an atmosphere of honest seeking and unrestricted discussion, we challenge you to put the claims of Jesus—as well as your own beliefs—to the test. And we trust you'll find *Experiencing the Passion of Jesus* to be a useful guide in facilitating this journey of spiritual discovery.

Of course, it is possible for any of us to believe error; it is also feasible for us to resist truth. Hopefully, this discussion guide will help you sort out truth from speculation, and facts from opinion. We're convinced it is healthy for all of us to wrestle with the assertions of the New Testament so we can make an informed decision about the relevance of Jesus to our personal lives.

THE PLACE FOR TOUGH QUESTIONS

Experiencing the Passion of Jesus is designed to give both spiritual seekers and Christians a chance to raise questions and investigate themes related to the death and resurrection of Jesus of Nazareth. If you have seen Mel Gibson's powerful and provocative film *The Passion of the Christ*, then undoubtedly issues have arisen in your mind concerning the identity of Jesus, why he endured the torture of the cross, and the implications of the resurrection. Your comments, questions, and concerns—even your objections—will be fully welcomed in the safe context of a small group discussion based on this guide.

Since the primary audience for this guide is the not-yet-convinced seekers, the ideal place to use *Experiencing the Passion of Jesus* is within the context of seeker small groups. These specialized groups consist of several people who are interested in investigating faith issues, along with a Christian or two who have volunteered to lead the discussions. These groups gather on a regular basis, perhaps weekly, at homes, offices, restaurants, churches—even Starbucks! The greatest hope behind the publication of this guide is that spiritual seekers everywhere will be encouraged in a respectful way to seriously consider the claims of Christ—and then to reach their own independent and well-informed decision about how to respond.

This guide is also designed for small groups of Christians to use as they discuss answers to the tough questions that skeptics and seekers are asking about Gibson's movie. The process of tackling these important issues will not only fortify their own faith, but it will also provide them with insights for entering into dialogues about Christianity with their seeking friends, colleagues, neighbors, and family members.

THE FEATURES

Experiencing the Passion of Jesus includes six discussion sessions, each with an introduction to the topic; ten to fifteen questions to draw out group interaction; several quotes to stimulate thinking; and Scripture references to provide additional biblical input. Your group may find it challenging to get through all the

You will seek me and find me when you seek me with all your heart.

JEREMIAH 29:13

material within each discussion in just one sitting. That's okay; the important thing is to engage in the topic at hand—not to necessarily get through every question. Your group, however, may decide to spend more than one meeting on each session in order to cover all the information addressed.

The discussion questions are intended to elicit spirited dialogue rather than short, simple answers. Strictly speaking, this guide is not a Bible study, though it regularly refers to biblical themes and passages. Instead, it is a topical discussion guide, meant to get you talking about what you really think and feel. The sessions have a point and attempt to lead to some resolution, but they fall short of providing the last word on any of the questions raised. That is left for you to discover for yourself! You will be invited to bring your experience, perspectives, and uncertainties to the discussion, and you will also be challenged to compare your beliefs with what the Bible teaches to determine where you stand as each meeting unfolds.

Each group should have a leader—not to lecture but to create an engaging experience in which all viewpoints are welcomed. *Seeker Small Groups* is recommended as a useful resource for leaders to learn how to effectively start up small groups and facilitate discussions for spiritual seekers. *The Complete Book of Questions: 1001 Conversation Starters for Any Occasion,* a resource filled with icebreaker questions, may be a helpful tool to assist everyone in your group to get to know one another better and more easily launch your group interactions.

In addition, keep the following list of suggestions in mind as you prepare to participate in your group discussions.

- Watch *The Passion of the Christ* together as a small group. You may also want to encourage other group members to read the sections from the Bible the film covers: Matthew 26:36–28:20; Mark 14:32–16:20; Luke 22:39–24:53; and John 18:1–21:25.

- If possible, read over the material to be discussed before each meeting. Familiarity with the topic will greatly enrich the time you spend in the discussion.

- It would be helpful for everyone to have a modern translation of the Bible, such as the New International Version. You might prefer to use a Bible that includes notes especially for seekers, such as *The Journey*.

- Be willing to join in the group interaction. The leader of the group will not present a sermon but will invite each of you to openly discuss your opinions and disagreements. Plan to share your ideas honestly and forthrightly.

- Be sensitive to the other members of your group. Listen attentively when they speak and be affirming whenever you can. This will motivate more hesitant members to participate. Always show respect toward the others, even if they don't agree with your position.

- Be careful not to dominate the discussion. Do participate but allow others to have equal time.

- Try to stick to the topic being studied. There won't be enough time to handle the peripheral matters that come to mind during your meeting. These might provide fodder, however, for further discussions outside the regular meeting.

- Do some extra reading in the Bible and other recommended books as you work through these sessions. To get you started, the "Scripture for Further Study" section lists several Bible references related to each topic, and the "Recommended Resources" section at the back of the guide offers ideas for books to read.

- One last suggestion: At the outset, even if you are not sure God exists, whisper a prayer. If you have doubts, tell him. If you're skeptical, let him know. But then ask him to reveal himself to you, and express your willingness to respond to him if and when he does.

THE CHALLENGE

Christianity stands or falls on Christ. And yet he left us with a lot of hard sayings. But the central scandal of Christianity is that at a point in history, God came down to live among us in a person, Jesus of Nazareth. And the most baffling moment of Jesus' life was on the cross, where he hung to die like a common criminal. In that place of weakness—where all seemed lost, where the taunts of "Prove yourself, Jesus, and come down from there!" lashed out like the whips that flogged him prior to his crucifixion—somehow God was at his best. There at the cross, he expressed a love greater than words could ever describe. That act of Jesus, presented as the ultimate demonstration of the love and justice of God, begs to be put to "cross" examination.

As you grapple with the most important event of history—the death and resurrection of Jesus—we are convinced you'll find satisfying, reasonable answers to your most challenging questions. And you are invited to discover them with others in your small group using this guide. Engage fully and sincerely with your whole heart and mind, and get ready for the adventure of a lifetime!

Seek and you will find; knock and the door will be opened to you.

MATTHEW 7:7

WHO *REALLY* KILLED JESUS?

Every trial is a quest to determine who committed the crime in question. Is the defendant responsible, or is some other person really at fault? Jurors listen to testimony and examine exhibits—a process that's often dry, tedious, and complicated by dense legalese. It is not uncommon to see jurors nodding off during the seemingly interminable pauses and delays.

But what if the jurors could see a videotape of the crime itself? The drama and intensity would certainly captivate them. The images would be much more compelling than the words that would be used later to describe what had happened.

The Passion of the Christ illustrates the ability of film to engage its audience. In shock and disbelief, repelled by the brutality and suffering, we witness the gruesome crucifixion of Jesus—and our instinct for justice is stirred. "Who did this?" we want to shout. "Who's to blame for this atrocity?" The endless flogging, the swollen eye, the shredded flesh—all of the horrific violence compels us to demand, "Who is responsible? Surely the guilty party must pay for this!"

Is Satan behind it all? Judas? Pilate? The religious leaders? The Roman soldiers? The screaming mob? For that matter, why didn't the disciples step in and try to stop the madness? A lot of people were involved, and yet we can't seem to figure out who's primarily responsible.

15

Pilate orders the unjust execution, and Roman troops carry it out with inhumane efficiency. The disciples scatter, except for Peter, who denies Jesus in the midst of the confusion and chaos. The chants from the crowd create a terrifying rhythm in the background, jeering each step of Jesus' journey to Golgotha and every slam of the hammer. Judas, the betrayer, hangs himself. The sinister presence of a shrouded Satan is haunting. He—or is it she?—is eerily delighted when Jesus is finally pronounced dead.

In that swarm of characters and commotion, where do we point our finger of blame? Suspicion and sensitivity run high as we explore the list of potential perpetrators.

Of course, the depiction of Jesus' death has always created controversy, whether it is told through medieval passion plays or the latest filmmaker's interpretation. Amazingly, newspapers carried stories about the debate over *The Passion of the Christ* months before the film was even released. One concern was that the movie—even unintentionally—would focus blame on Jews collectively, vilifying them and encouraging anti-Semitism.

What is the truth behind the death of Jesus? Who are the real culprits? Our sense of justice requires a verdict. Maybe if we expose who is really to blame, we'll begin to make some sense out of the apparently senseless horror.

Open for Discussion

1. Name the movies you have seen that have dealt with the story of Jesus. Which one was the most powerful? Why?

2. What impact did *The Passion of the Christ* have on you? How did it inspire or surprise you?

3. What did you like most and least about the film? Which scene is most memorable for you?

4. Religious upbringing, the media, comments of friends, and even motion pictures can raise questions in our minds about Jesus. What questions or doubts are especially pressing to you?

In fact, if Christ himself stood in my way, I, like Nietzsche, would not hesitate to squish him like a worm.

CHE GUEVARA

5. Have you ever witnessed someone being treated unfairly and felt an intense desire for the perpetrator to be held accountable? Describe what happened.

6. How did *The Passion of the Christ* change your opinion about who was most responsible for Jesus' death? Who would you say the movie portrays as being guilty? Why?

7. What difference does it make who killed Jesus? How important is it to *you* to know who killed Jesus? Why?

8. How are the allegations concerning anti-Semitism supported or weakened by the fact that Jesus was Jewish, his closest friends and followers were all Jewish, he lived in a Jewish community, and he was hailed as a hero by Jewish crowds as he entered Jerusalem on Palm Sunday?

9. Take a few moments to read the verses below. Then, based on what those references suggest, complete the chart by listing the possible

I lay down my life—only to take it up again. No one takes it from me, but I lay it down of my own accord. I have authority to lay it down and authority to take it up again. This command I received from my Father.

JESUS CHRIST

accomplices to Jesus' death. How does your list clarify or confuse the issue for you?

Bible verses	Accomplices
Matthew 26:47–49	
Matthew 27:1	
Matthew 27:20–22	
Matthew 27:26	
Matthew 27:27–31	
Matthew 27:46	
Luke 22:3–4	
John 10:17–18	

10. Read the following Bible passages. Given the tension between God's sovereignty and human responsibility, who do you think the Bible claims is *ultimately* responsible for Jesus' death?

"Where do you come from?" [Pilate] asked Jesus, but Jesus gave him no answer. "Do you refuse to speak to me?" Pilate said. "Don't you realize I have power either to free you or to crucify you?"

Jesus answered, "You would have no power over me if it were not given to you from above."

John 19:9–11

[Jesus], being in very nature God, did not consider equality with God something to be grasped, but made himself nothing, taking the very nature of a servant, being made in human likeness. And being found in appearance as a man, he humbled himself and became obedient to death—even death on a cross!

Philippians 2:6–8

Do you think I cannot call on my Father, and he will at once put at my disposal more than twelve legions of angels? But how then would the Scriptures be fulfilled that say it must happen in this way?

JESUS CHRIST

But God demonstrates his own love for us in this: While we were still sinners, Christ died for us.

Romans 5:8

He himself bore our sins in his body on the tree, so that we might die to sins and live for righteousness; by his wounds you have been healed.

1 Peter 2:24

My sins were the first to nail him to the cross.

MEL GIBSON

11. Do you agree with this statement made by Billy Graham after he saw *The Passion of the Christ*: "The film is faithful to the Bible's teaching that we are all responsible for Jesus' death, because we have all sinned. It is our sins that caused his death, not any particular group"? In what sense do you think we are responsible since we had not even been born when Jesus was crucified?

12. Check the statement(s) below that best describes your position at this point. Share your selection with the rest of the group and offer some reasons for your response.

_____ I'm not sure why the question of who killed Jesus is relevant.

_____ I'm convinced no single group of people alone is responsible for Jesus' death.

_____ I understand the Bible teaches we are all responsible for Jesus' death, but I'm not sure I believe it.

_____ I believe my sin and the sins of the world crucified Jesus.

_____ I believe the specific characters identified in the Bible each had a role in Jesus' death.

_____ I have all kinds of doubts about God, because it doesn't make sense to me that he would simply stand back and allow his son to be murdered without stepping in to stop it.

_____ I'm confused about how I could somehow be responsible for Jesus' death.

_____ Write your own phrase here: _____
_____
_____

> When you look at the reasons behind why Christ came, why he was crucified, he died and suffered for all mankind, so that, really, anybody who transgresses has to look at their own part in his death.
>
> MEL GIBSON

Scripture for Further Study

- Acts 2:22–24
- Romans 3:9–12, 21–26
- Romans 5:6–8
- 2 Corinthians 5:21
- Philippians 2:6–11
- 1 Peter 2:22–25

WHAT CRIME DID
JESUS COMMIT?

Lionel Tate was twelve years old when he tried out some wrestling moves he saw on television on a playmate. Tragedy ensued—a six-year-old girl was killed, and Tate found himself being tried as an adult on a charge of first-degree murder. Declared guilty, he was automatically given a sentence of life in prison.

The nation was shocked by both his crime and his punishment. Tate's lawyer called the death an accident and said it was simply unjust to lock up a child for the rest of his life, with no possibility of release. The appeals court later overturned the conviction, and Tate agreed to plead guilty to second-degree murder. His final sentence was three years in detention, a year of house arrest, and ten years of probation.

Our sensibilities are shocked when the punishment doesn't fit the crime. Certainly it is only fair that the severity of the punishment reflect the seriousness of the offense. Let your parking meter run out and you deserve a small fine. Break the speed limit too many times or drive drunk, and your license will be suspended. Shoplift and you might receive a sentence of community service or a month in the county lockup. If you're arrested for selling drugs to minors, you could do lengthy prison time. And if you kill someone, you could be given a life sentence or the ultimate penalty.

When Roman officials handed down Jesus' sentence, it was a harsh one—death. But Jesus' punishment was not a simple, swift execution; he was condemned to die on a cross. In ancient Rome, crucifixion was designed to be a combination of physical torture and psychological humiliation, as well as a warning to other would-be criminals not to step out of line. This death penalty was reserved for the most heinous of criminals—traitors to the Roman Empire, insurrectionists, and murderers.

Jesus' punishment involved torture that lasted for hours. People spit in his face, struck him with their fists, and hurled insults at him. He endured the mocking ceremony of a thorny crown being shoved onto his skull. Then he endured beatings so severe that they left gaping wounds. A third-century historian named Eusebius describes a Roman flogging: "The sufferer's veins were laid bare, and the very muscles, sinews, and bowels of the victim were open to exposure."

Later, Jesus staggered under the weight of the very cross upon which he would be nailed. As he was winding up the road to the place of his execution, he collapsed, unable to take another step. A member of the crowd, Simon from Cyrene, was pressed into service to carry it the rest of the way to Golgotha. Finally, Jesus was affixed to the cross and left to die.

Jesus' crime must have been horrific to warrant such abuse. The Roman soldiers, religious leaders, the venomous mob—everyone boiled with wrath toward him.

But exactly what had Jesus done to deserve this? Surely he wouldn't have been so aggressively condemned if he hadn't done something truly reprehensible. What crime did he commit? Why was he crucified? What was the real reason Jesus was sentenced to this gruesome death?

Open for Discussion ──────────────

1. If Jesus came into our world today, how do you think people would react and respond to him?

2. What crimes, if any, do you believe warrant a death sentence?

3. Read the following Bible passage. Why do you think Pilate had such a difficult time deciding what to do with Jesus? What riled up the crowd so much that they demanded Jesus be crucified?

Then the whole assembly rose and led him off to Pilate. And they began to accuse him, saying, "We have found this man subverting our nation. He opposes payment of taxes to Caesar and claims to be Christ, a king."

So Pilate asked Jesus, "Are you the king of the Jews?"

"Yes, it is as you say," Jesus replied.

Then Pilate announced to the chief priests and the crowd, "I find no basis for a charge against this man."

Pilate had a notice prepared and fastened to the cross. It read: JESUS OF NAZARETH, THE KING OF THE JEWS . . . The sign was written in Aramaic, Latin and Greek. The chief priests of the Jews protested to Pilate, "Do not write 'The King of the Jews,' but that this man claimed to be king of the Jews." Pilate answered, "What I have written, I have written."

JOHN 19:19–22

But they insisted, "He stirs up the people all over Judea by his teaching. He started in Galilee and has come all the way here."

... Pilate called together the chief priests, the rulers and the people, and said to them, "You brought me this man as one who was inciting the people to rebellion. I have examined him in your presence and have found no basis for your charges against him. Neither has Herod, for he sent him back to us; as you can see, he has done nothing to deserve death. Therefore, I will punish him and then release him."

With one voice they cried out, "Away with this man! Release Barabbas to us!" (Barabbas had been thrown into prison for an insurrection in the city, and for murder.)

Wanting to release Jesus, Pilate appealed to them again. But they kept shouting, "Crucify him! Crucify him!"

For the third time he spoke to them: "Why? What crime has this man committed? I have found in him no grounds for the death penalty. Therefore I will have him punished and then release him."

But with loud shouts they insistently demanded that he be crucified, and their shouts prevailed. So Pilate decided to grant their demand. He released the man who had been thrown into prison for insurrection and murder, the one they asked for, and surrendered Jesus to their will.

Luke 23:1–5, 13–25

> For we do not have a high priest who is unable to sympathize with our weaknesses, but we have one who has been tempted in every way, just as we are—yet was without sin.
>
> HEBREWS 4:15

4. According to John 19:12 the crowd kept shouting, "If you let this man go, you are no friend of Caesar. Anyone who claims to be a king opposes Caesar." Why do you think Jesus was a political threat to the Romans?

5. Why do you think Jesus was treated with so much hatred and animosity?

> "You do not want to leave too, do you?" Jesus asked the Twelve.
>
> Simon Peter answered him, "Lord, to whom shall we go? You have the words of eternal life. We believe and know that you are the Holy One of God.
>
> JOHN 6:67–69

6. Do you think Jesus deserved to die? Why or why not?

7. Read Mark 15:3–5 below. Why do you suppose Jesus defended himself the way he did?

The chief priests accused him of many things. So again Pilate asked him, "Aren't you going to answer? See how many things they are accusing you of."

But Jesus still made no reply, and Pilate was amazed.

Mark 15:2–5

8. According to the following Bible verses, what appears to be the crime Jesus was guilty of committing? What charges were leveled against him?

The high priest said to him, "I charge you under oath by the living God: Tell us if you are the Christ, the Son of God."

"Yes, it is as you say," Jesus replied. "But I say to all of you: In the future you will see the Son of Man sitting at the right hand of the Mighty One and coming on the clouds of heaven."

Then the high priest tore his clothes and said, "He has spoken blasphemy! Why do we need any more witnesses? Look, now you have heard the blasphemy. What do you think?"

"He is worthy of death," they answered.

Then they spit in his face and struck him with their fists. Others slapped him and said, "Prophesy to us, Christ. Who hit you?"

Matthew 26:63–68

The Jews insisted, "We have a law, and according to that law he must die, because he claimed to be the Son of God."

John 19:7

"Yes, Lord," she told him, "I believe that you are the Christ, the Son of God, who was to come into the world."

MARTHA

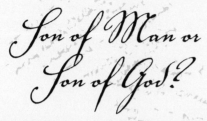
Son of Man or Son of God?

Some people think Jesus only believed he was a man, because he refers to himself four dozen times in the gospels as the Son of Man. They say, "See! He only claimed to be a human being!"

However, Jesus was applying Daniel 7:13–14 to himself. Here, the Son of Man is portrayed as a divine figure who has authority, glory, and sovereign power, who receives the worship of all people, and who will come at the end of the world to judge humankind and rule forever.

"Thus," said theologian William Lane Craig, "the claim to be the Son of Man would be in effect a claim to divinity."

---

9. *Blasphemy* is defined as contemptuous or irreverent talk about God. What prompted the religious leaders to accuse Jesus of blasphemy?

10. According to the following verses, did Jesus really claim to be God? Do you think Jesus actually believed himself to be God? Explain.

Then came the Feast of Dedication at Jerusalem. It was winter, and Jesus was in the temple area walking in Solomon's Colonnade. The Jews gathered around him, saying, "How long will you keep us in suspense? If you are the Christ, tell us plainly."

Jesus answered, "I did tell you, but you do not believe. The miracles I do in my Father's name speak for me, but you do not believe because you are not my sheep. My sheep listen to my voice; I

> For he received honor and glory from God the Father when the voice came to him from the Majestic Glory, saying, "This is my Son, whom I love; with him I am well pleased."
>
> 2 PETER 1:17

know them, and they follow me. I give them eternal life, and they shall never perish; no one can snatch them out of my hand. My Father, who has given them to me, is greater than all; no one can snatch them out of my Father's hand. I and the Father are one."

Again the Jews picked up stones to stone him, but Jesus said to them, "I have shown you many great miracles from the Father. For which of these do you stone me?"

"We are not stoning you for any of these," replied the Jews, "but for blasphemy, because you, a mere man, claim to be God."

John 10:22–33

> If Jesus Christ is only a human being—no matter how splendid a specimen of humanity he may be—he is part of the problem, not its solution.
>
> ALISTER MCGRATH

11. Anyone can claim to be God, but Jesus actually convinced his followers that he was telling the truth about his divine identity. He did this by

- performing miracles (both the Jewish Talmud and Islamic Koran concede he performed supernatural acts);
- living a sinless life (two of his closest companions, John and Peter, observed his moral perfection; see 1 John 3:5 and 1 Peter 2:22);
- fulfilling ancient Messianic prophecies against all mathematical odds;
- and his resurrection from the dead.

Do you believe these arguments are sufficient to establish that Jesus was God incarnate? Why or why not?

12. Indicate which statement(s) you think best describes who Jesus was. Offer some reasons for your response.

Jesus was . . .

_____ an insane man who thought he was a god

_____ a fool

_____ a good man who was confused about his true identity

_____ the Son of God (God in human form)

_____ a criminal deserving of death

_____ a prophet

_____ a righteous man without sin

_____ a good but imperfect man

_____ a wise religious teacher

_____ a teacher who deceived others about his true identity

_____ a legend—he never existed

> Either this man was, and is, the Son of God: or else a madman or something worse. You can shut him up for a fool, you can spit at him and kill him as a demon; or you can fall at his feet and call him Lord and God. But let us not come with any patronizing nonsense about him being a great human teacher. He has not left that open to us. He did not intend to.
>
> C. S. LEWIS

13. Check the statement(s) below that best describes your position at this point. Share your selection with the rest of the group and give reasons for your response.

_____ Jesus deserved to die.

_____ Jesus was completely innocent of all wrongdoing.

_____ Jesus was condemned for claiming to be God and threatening to establish a kingdom.

_____ Jesus never really claimed to be God.

_____ I am unsure what to believe about who Jesus was.

_____ I am convinced that Jesus was exactly who he claimed to be—God in a human body.

_____ Jesus claimed to be God, but I am certain he was mistaken.

_____ Write your own phrase here: _____

_____

_____

> Jesus made it clear by word and deed that to know him was to know God, to see him was to see God, to believe in him was to believe in God, to receive him was to receive God, to reject him was to reject God, and to honor him was to honor God.
>
> JOHN STOTT

Scripture for Further Study

- Matthew 26:1–5, 47–68
- Matthew 27:11–31
- Mark 14:43–65
- Mark 15:1–15
- Luke 22:66–71
- Luke 23:1–25
- John 14:6
- John 18:19–24, 28–40
- John 19:1–16

DID IT ACTUALLY HAPPEN LIKE THAT?

"What if . . . ?" This question catalyzes the imagination. Writers and directors dream this and then draft stories that frequently blur the line between true life and fiction. Locations are real, though characters are make-believe. Events are factual, but fanciful themes and conflicts are woven in. We are drawn into these worlds and find ourselves willingly accepting these cinematic versions of reality.

Take, for instance, James Cameron's movie *Titanic*. Screenwriters crafted the primary plot—a fictitious romance—for dramatic interest. At the same time, designers were historically accurate in re-creating the ship's lavish layout, dinnerware, lighting, and décor. So the love story between Jack and Rose that dominated the film was a work of fiction played against the backdrop of a tragic historical event. We're left to wonder how much of the movie is actually true.

Another example is Oliver Stone's film *JFK*, which many accused of irresponsibly mingling conjecture, rumor, and half-truths with the real-life issue of who assassinated President John Kennedy. The final product leaves viewers confused about where wild conspiracy theories leave off and solid history begins.

What about *The Passion of the Christ*? Did Jesus' death really unfold like that? How much of this story is real? Most of us know the basic contours of what happened to Jesus, but is the film's accuracy tainted by speculations spun from the question "What if ... ?"

Other writers also have started with the central details of Jesus' life and, taking dramatic license, let their creativity run wild. Some results are captivating, others are thought-provoking, and a few are controversial. Musicals such as *Jesus Christ Superstar* and *Godspell* present a very different Jesus than the one in Martin Scorsese's *The Last Temptation of Christ* or the bestselling novel *The Da Vinci Code*. What's factual and what's fabricated?

There are ways to discern what parts of *Titanic* are true. We could search historical records that date back to the event itself, before legend could have corrupted them. We might find photos that show how well the filmmaker re-created the actual dinnerware. And we'd search for the passenger list to find out who was simply a figment of the screenwriter's imagination.

Similarly, there are ways to find out about the essential accuracy of *The Passion of the Christ*. By checking the primary source for the script, the gospels found in the New Testament of the Bible, we could determine whether the details and characters of the film diverge from the record.

Yet more questions come to mind. Even if the film strictly adhered to the Bible, how do we know that the New Testament is reliable and not merely an embellished fable? It is, after all, nearly two thousand years old. That's a long time to keep details straight.

Besides, were the authors of the Bible striving for historical accuracy, or did they just want to tell a good story? Did they fabricate claims, such as the divinity of Jesus, to fulfill their own wishful thinking? Is it possible that the writers of the Bible were blurring the line between fact and fiction?

Now it's your turn. What if you actually investigated the Bible for yourself? What if you scrutinized the text to determine its authenticity and reliability? You just might discover the truth behind the passion of Jesus.

Open for Discussion ———————————

1. What do you like and dislike most about movies that are based on true stories? What is one of your favorite films in this genre, and why do you like it?

2. Compare and contrast *The Passion of the Christ* with what you already knew about the life and death of Jesus Christ. Which parts of the movie do you believe are based on conjecture, and which parts do you think are based on facts?

> **It is as it was.**
>
> POPE JOHN PAUL II
> alleged comment after
> viewing *The Passion
> of the Christ*

3. Using the scale below, indicate the degree you believe the events depicted in *The Passion of the Christ* actually occurred. Explain your response.

1	2	3	4	5	6	7	8	9	10
I am very certain few of the events actually occurred.				I am unsure which, if any, of the events actually occurred.				I am very certain most of the events actually occurred.	

What Is Truth?

The basic meaning of the Hebrew word normally translated as "truth" or "true" (as in "the true God") is "something which can be relied upon" or "someone who can be trusted." Truth thus is not simply about being right. It is about trustworthiness. It is a relational concept, pointing us to someone who is totally worthy of our trust.

ALISTER MCGRATH

Just before Jesus was sentenced to be crucified, a private moment occurred between Jesus and Pilate, as recorded in John 18:37: "You are a king, then!" said Pilate.

Jesus answered, "You are right in saying I am a king. In fact, for this reason I was born, and for this I came into the world, to testify to the truth. Everyone on the side of truth listens to me."

Afterward, Pilate is left with one haunting question: What is truth?

4. How would you answer Pilate's question "What is truth?"

5. Do you think it is possible to know what is true and what is not? Or is it futile to even try to understand truth from falsehood? Explain your response.

6. Friedrich Nietzsche said, "There are no facts, only interpretations." What are some of the logical implications if he were correct? Is Nietzsche's statement a fact or an interpretation?

DISCUSSION THREE
36

7. Consider the last time you read a story in a newspaper or magazine or on the Internet. Which of the factors listed below determined whether you believed the incident was true or false? Indicate which factors you routinely use to evaluate whether someone's story is accurate?

_____ The character and trustworthiness of the author(s)

_____ The time elapsed since the event occured

_____ The medium by which the event is conveyed

_____ The potential personal benefit to the author or publication

_____ The personal bias or agenda of the author or publication

_____ The attitude or emotion behind the words

_____ Whether there are other witnesses or corroborating evidence that confirms or contradicts the event

_____ Whether other supporting details in the story are accurate

_____ Whether the story includes details that aren't necessarily flattering to the author(s)

_____ Whether parts of the story contradict each other

_____ Other factors

After watching *The Passion of the Christ*, I feel as if I have actually been there. I was moved to tears. I doubt if there has ever been a more graphic and moving presentation of Jesus' death and resurrection—which Christians believe are the most important events in human history.

BILLY GRAHAM

The Reliability of the Biblical Record

Can we trust what the New Testament tells us about what Jesus said and did? Many scholars agree that the ancient historical documents that make up the New Testament are trustworthy because of three strands of evidence:

They are *early* accounts. The central tenets of the Christian faith are confirmed by texts that date back so close to Jesus' life that their credibility could not have been wiped out by legendary development. Also, the gospels and the apostle Paul's letters were circulating during the lifetimes of Jesus' contemporaries, who would have disputed their contents if they were exaggerated or false.

They are rooted in *eyewitness* testimony. The New Testament contains accounts that can be traced to the disciples Matthew, John, and Peter; James and Paul, both skeptics who became believers after encountering the resurrected Christ; John Mark, a companion of the eyewitness Peter; and Luke, a close friend of Paul's and a sort of first-century investigative reporter. Peter writes: "We did not follow cleverly invented stories when we told you about the power and coming of our Lord Jesus Christ, but we were eyewitnesses of his majesty" (2 Peter 1:16).

They have the *earmarks* of authenticity. Archaeology has repeatedly established that Luke, who wrote a quarter of the New Testament, was a careful and accurate historian. Also, the gospels contain difficult-to-explain sayings by Jesus and embarrassing material about the disciples—their cowardice, unbelief, and grandiosity— that surely would have been edited out if the writers wanted to whitewash the record. Finally, in his book *The Historical Jesus,* scholar Gary Habermas examines evidence for Jesus outside the Bible and details a total of thirty-nine ancient sources from which he enumerates more than one hundred reported facts about Christ's life, teachings, crucifixion, and resurrection.

8. Do you believe the New Testament contains an accurate account of what really happened to Jesus? Why or why not? On which factors, if any (identified above and in question 7), do you base your response?

The Credibility of a Creed

One of the earliest creeds recited by Christians (found in 1 Corinthians 15) affirms that "Christ died for our sins according to the Scriptures," that he was buried, and that he rose on the third day. It then mentions specific eyewitnesses, including skeptics, who encountered him. Scholars have dated this creed back to as early as two to eight years after Jesus' crucifixion—too soon to have been rendered unreliable by mythological development, according to classical historian A. N. Sherwin-White of Oxford University.

9. In light of the above information about the 1 Corinthians 15 creed, are you more or less likely to believe that the tenets of Christianity were the result of legend or wishful thinking? Explain your answer.

Jesus Outside the Bible

How much can we know about Jesus from ancient sources *outside* the Bible? Quite a bit, says historian Edwin Yamauchi of Miami University:

"We would know that first, Jesus was a Jewish teacher; second, many people believed that he performed healings and exorcisms; third, some people believed he was the Messiah; fourth, he was rejected by the Jewish leaders; fifth, he was crucified under Pontius Pilate in the reign of Tiberius; sixth, despite his shameful death, his followers, who believed that he was still alive, spread beyond Palestine so that there were multitudes of them in Rome by AD 64; and seventh, all kinds of people from the cities and countryside—men and women, slave and free—worshiped him as God."

10. To what extent have you examined the evidence for the life, death, and resurrection of Christ in sources outside the Bible? How much influence do outside sources have on your belief in the biblical accounts of Jesus?

Nobody Dies for a Lie

It has been said that people will die for their religious beliefs if they sincerely think they're true, but people won't die for their religious beliefs if they know their beliefs are false. Consider that in all of history, Jesus' disciples were in a unique position to know for a fact whether Jesus did, indeed, return from the dead. They were willing to face torture and death, but they never disavowed their claim that Jesus was the unique Son of God who proved his divinity by his resurrection. As Josh McDowell has said, nobody knowingly and willingly dies for a lie.

11. In your view, how does the information above affect the credibility of the disciples' testimony? Explain.

12. On a scale from one to ten, place an X on the continuum near the phrase that best describes what you believe about the Bible. What reasons do you have for placing your X where you did?

1	2	3	4	5	6	7	8	9	10

The Bible is
filled with
myths and
fables.

The Bible
mixes fact
and fiction.

The Bible
is totally
reliable.

13. Check the statement(s) that best describes your position at this point. Share your selection with the rest of the group and give reasons for your response.

_____ I'm not convinced the Bible contains an accurate depiction of what really happened.

_____ I think the Bible is a combination of historical facts and fables.

_____ I believe the Bible for the most part, but I still have my doubts.

_____ I think that the Bible is sufficiently accurate.

_____ I'm unsure what to believe, but I'd like to learn more.

_____ I think the Bible is a mythological tale concocted by people with an agenda.

_____ I think the Bible is the product of wishful thinking by sincere people.

_____ Write your own phrase here: _____

_____

_____

Scripture for Further Study

- 1 Corinthians 15:3–8
- 2 Timothy 3:16
- Hebrews 4:12
- 2 Peter 1:16–18
- 1 John 1:1–3

WHY DID JESUS SUFFER AND DIE?

Life without purpose is empty, futile, hopeless. "The greatest tragedy is not death," says our friend Rick Warren, "but life without purpose."

Warren helps people understand that we derive our ultimate purpose from God. "Knowing your purpose gives meaning to your life," he says. "When life has meaning, you can bear almost anything; without it, nothing is bearable."

Few circumstances are more heartbreaking than someone losing their life in some senseless mishap. On the other hand, people are comforted—even inspired— by those who sacrifice their life for a great and noble cause.

When a military commander meets with the mourning parents of a soldier killed in action, he seeks to persuade them that their son or daughter's sacrifice was not in vain. There's reassurance in knowing that he or she died while valiantly saving the life of a friend, liberating an oppressed village, or contributing to the demise of a blood-thirsty tyrant.

Did Jesus' life—and death—really have meaning? Was any purpose served by his horrific execution? Why did he have to suffer and die?

In the Garden of Gethsemane, a stone's throw away from his disciples, Jesus knelt down and prayed, whispering the words of an intimate struggle: "My Father, if it is possible, may this cup be taken from me." Can he avoid what's ahead? Is there any alternative to this gruesome plan?

But the Father has a purpose for his death. Resolved to fully submit to him, Jesus utters, "Yet not as I will, but as you will." His words seal his fate. The plan is set in motion. Judas betrays him with a kiss, and the suffering and pain ensue—a savage festival of violence and inhumanity.

Even after his scourging at the hands of brutal soldiers, even after the jeering and catcalls of the crowd, even after the crown of thorns, there's more. Nails pounded through his hands and feet. An agonizingly slow death by crucifixion—essentially, Jesus is gradually asphyxiated on the cross.

Hanging in a vertical position exerted stress on his intercostal, pectoral, and deltoid muscles, putting his lungs into an inhaling position. To exhale, he needed to push up to ease the tension on his muscles. The nail would tear through his feet, locking against the tarsal bones, and his bloodied back would scrape against the rough-hewn cross. He would manage to exhale, then relax down as he took another breath.

Eventually, exhaustion set in. His breathing slowed. The acidity of his blood increased, prompting an erratic heartbeat. At that point, knowing death was occurring, Jesus said, "Father, into your hands I commit my spirit," and then he died of cardiac arrest. Literally, a broken heart.

Humiliation, torture, death. Was this really God's perfect plan for his life? Was everything that happened to Jesus exactly what God wanted? Every slap, whip, and kick? Every insult? All the abuse? The pounding of each nail? The shedding of so much blood?

Was there no other way to fulfill his divine will? If not, was the *degree* of suffering necessary? It doesn't seem to make sense. Surely no good can come of such violence. Jesus suffered too much.

Why did Jesus have to walk this road? What purpose, if any, did his death actually serve? What in the world was God thinking he would accomplish?

Open for Discussion

1. "Life without purpose is empty, futile, hopeless." Do you agree or disagree with this statement? Give reasons for your response.

2. Given the graphic nature of *The Passion of the Christ*, how did you react to the depiction of the crucifixion of Christ? Did you feel that the movie was too graphic? Why or why not?

Sweating Blood?

Skeptics often scoff at the Bible's claim that prior to his flogging and crucifixion, Jesus sweat blood while praying in the Garden of Gethsemane. Some attribute this dramatic detail to the overactive imaginations of the gospel writers.

An expert on the crucifixion, Dr. Alexander Metherell, however, says this is a known medical condition called *hematidrosis*, which is associated with a high degree of psychological stress.

"Severe anxiety causes the release of chemicals that break down the capillaries in the sweat glands," he says. "As a result, there's a small amount of bleeding into these glands, and the sweat comes out tinged with blood."

This also has another effect: "What this did was to set up the skin to be extremely fragile so that when Jesus was flogged, his skin would be very, very sensitive."

3. *The Passion of the Christ* was emotionally heavy due to the torturous way Jesus was treated. What was the most painful part for you to watch? What do you think was the most painful thing for him to endure?

4. How would you react to the soldiers if they were abusing, humiliating, and torturing you, as they did Jesus?

A New Word

The torture of the cross was so incredibly painful that it was beyond words to describe. A new word had to be coined: *excruciating* literally means "out of the cross."

5. Assuming God is ultimately in control (sovereign), why do you believe he allowed Jesus to suffer such a horrible death?

6. What could possibly account for Jesus' prayer in the midst of his agony, "Father, forgive them"? Do you think you would have been able to do the same? Why or why not?

7. In your opinion, what was Jesus Christ's ultimate reason for coming to this world?

> Christ forgave even as he was tortured and killed. That's the ultimate example of love.
>
> MEL GIBSON

Born to Die

There is no doubt that Jesus was on a mission when he lived among us—a role that only he could fulfill. His whole purpose in coming into our world was to give his life so we might live. More than his teaching, more than his example, he was God's rescue operation on earth. Read the following verses to see just how clearly the Bible spells out his mission:

Jesus took the Twelve aside and told them, "We are going up to Jerusalem, and everything that is written by the prophets about the Son of Man will be fulfilled. He will be handed over to the Gentiles. They will mock him, insult him, spit on him, flog him, and kill him. On the third day he will rise again."

Luke 18:31–33

Surely he took up our infirmities and carried our sorrows, yet we considered him stricken by God, smitten by him, and afflicted. But he was pierced for our transgressions, he was crushed for our iniquities; the punishment that

> Like a father saying about his sick child, "I'd do anything to make you well," God finally calls his own bluff and does it. Jesus Christ is what God does, and the cross [is] where he did it.
>
> FREDERICK BUECHNER

brought us peace was upon him, and by his wounds we are healed. We all, like sheep, have gone astray, each of us has turned to his own way; and the Lord has laid on him the iniquity of us all.

Isaiah 53:4–6
(foretelling the crucifixion more than 600 years in advance)

The Son of Man did not come to be served, but to serve, and to give his life as a ransom for many.

Matthew 20:28

[Jesus Christ] is the atoning sacrifice for our sins, and not only for ours but also for the sins of the whole world.

1 John 2:2

In him we have redemption through his blood, the forgiveness of sins, in accordance with the riches of God's grace that he lavished on us with all wisdom and understanding.

Ephesians 1:7–8

This is love: not that we loved God, but that he loved us and sent his Son as an atoning sacrifice for our sins.

1 John 4:10

How could God permit [the crucifixion of Jesus Christ] ...? The deranged reason of the little community found quite a frightfully absurd answer: God gave his Son for forgiveness, as a sacrifice ... The sacrifice for guilt, and just in its most repugnant and barbarous form—the sacrifice of the innocent for the sins of the guilty! What horrifying heathenism!

FRIEDRICH NIETZSCHE

8. Jesus' death wasn't accidental; it was an intentional and divine strategy. Based on the verses above, what do you think the Bible teaches regarding the purpose of Jesus' death? Do you agree with this teaching? Why or why not?

9. How might it be possible that Jesus' death is a sufficient "atoning sacrifice for our sins"?

10. Do you agree or disagree with the following statement? Explain.

   If there is any other way to bring us to God, then Jesus died in vain. But he died on our behalf because he was the only one worthy to make full payment for our sins. Any other conclusion makes a mockery out of Jesus' death.

> For the good news is not just that God became man, nor that God has spoken to reveal a proper way of life for us, nor even that death, the great enemy, is conquered. Rather, the good news is that sin has been dealt with (of which the resurrection is a proof); that Jesus has suffered its penalty for us as our representative, so that we might never have to suffer it; and that therefore all who believe in him can look forward to heaven.
>
> JAMES MONTGOMERY BOICE

11. Assuming it is true that Jesus needed to die in order to atone (make payment) for all of our sins, what reasons can you give for the extreme suffering of Jesus? In other words, was there any significance behind a brutal and agonizing death as opposed to a swift and painless death? Explain.

12. Read the following verse. Would you be willing to suffer for the sake of another person? For whom and why? What would it take to motivate you to endure torture in the place of someone else?

> You see, at just the right time, when we were still powerless, Christ died for the ungodly. Very rarely will anyone die for a righteous man, though for a good man someone might possibly dare to die. But God demonstrates his own love for us in this: While we were still sinners, Christ died for us.
>
> Romans 5:6–8

By the cross we know the gravity of sin and the greatness of God's love towards us.

JOHN CHRYSOSTOM

13. How do you feel about the idea that Jesus paid the price for all sin—including yours—and that he died for you?

14. Check the statement(s) below that best describes your position at this point. Share your selection with the rest of the group and give reasons for your response.

_____ I am not convinced Jesus had to die in order for God to forgive us of our sins.

_____ I'm still uncertain of the significance of Jesus' death.

_____ I think I believe that Jesus died on my behalf, but I don't understand it.

_____ I am certain Jesus died on my behalf.

_____ I understand what the Bible teaches about the significance of Jesus' death, but I don't buy it.

_____ It seems cruel to me that God would allow his son to suffer so much.

_____ I don't understand how one death could possibly cover all the sins throughout all the ages.

_____ Write your own phrase here: _____

_____

_____

> Greater love has no one than this, that he lay down his life for his friends.
>
> JOHN 15:13

Scripture for Further Study

- Isaiah 53:10–12
- Luke 19:10
- 1 Corinthians 15:3
- Hebrews 2:9–10, 17–18
- Hebrews 5:7–10
- Hebrews 9:22, 27–28
- Hebrews 10:12

WHAT DID THE RESURRECTION ACCOMPLISH?

Powerful thunder cracks overhead like colossal whips. The earth seems possessed, quivering and then convulsing underfoot. Some unseen force slashes the temple curtain from top to bottom. A terrified soldier shouts in awe, "Surely he was the Son of God!" For a time, darkness blankets the confusion, as if all are buried alive . . .

. . . all except one. There is one who has breathed his last. For him, it is finished. It is finally finished. The pandemonium fades. The spectators disperse. The earth settles.

Stillness.

Silence.

Clean linen, a new tomb in a quiet garden, a huge stone. The Sabbath invites those who love him to wait, to rest. For Jesus, there is ultimate rest—from the pain, the suffering, the degradation. No more whips against the back or strikes to the face. No more beatings or bruises. The sentence has been carried out. The debt to society has been paid. It is done. It's over.

Or is it?

Early morning, the first day of the week, Mary Magdalene goes to the tomb with some other women.

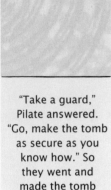

"Take a guard," Pilate answered. "Go, make the tomb as secure as you know how." So they went and made the tomb secure by putting a seal on the stone and posting the guard.

MATTHEW 27:65–66

But wait. The stone is rolled back. The strips of linen are laid aside, the burial cloth folded neatly by itself. The tomb . . . it's empty!

His body is gone—he's not there! Two men gleaming like lightning stand beside the trembling women. "Why do you look for the living among the dead? He is not here; he has risen!"

Risen?

They rush to the disciples to tell them the news. He's risen—he's alive!—just as he had foretold. Peter and John race to the tomb and find it just as the women said: Empty. Jesus is gone!

Where is he?

Jesus shows up everywhere. He spends time with Mary, two others on the road to Emmaus, and then Peter and the disciples. After that, he even appears to a group of five hundred. He cooks breakfast for his friends. He talks. He eats some fish. He is very much alive. They still wonder, *Is it really true?*

"Why are you troubled, and why do doubts rise in your minds?" he asks them. "Look at my hands and my feet. It is I myself! Touch me and see; a ghost does not have flesh and bones, as you see I have." They still find it hard to believe despite their joy and amazement! *It can't be . . . can it? Can he really and truly be alive?*

Yes, it's him! Without question, this is his body. The marks of the crucifixion are still evident: the nail-punctured hands and feet, the pierced side. How can he be alive after all that physical torment? How can he be walking around, talking with people, eating a broiled fish?

He patiently extends an invitation to Thomas, the doubter: "Put your finger here; see my hands. Reach out your hand and put it into my side. Stop doubting and believe."

Thomas does. The doubter touches, sees—and believes. "My Lord and my God!" Thomas exclaims, convinced that this is Jesus, the one he saw crucified, dead, and buried. And the one who rose again on the third day exactly as he said he would. Now here he is, healed, though scarred, and standing alive before them all.

So the dead hero comes back to life. How about that—a storybook ending! Everyone's delighted. At least, Jesus and his friends are. And that's that, right? All's well that ends well. Close the book and move on.

Right?

Open for Discussion

1. If you were writing the story of Jesus, how might you have ended it differently?

2. Do you believe in life after death? Why or why not? On what do you base your opinion?

Christ has turned all our sunsets into dawns.

CLEMENT OF ALEXANDER

We have never seen, in our time, nature go out of her course; but we have good reason to believe that millions of lies have been told in the same time; it is, therefore, at least millions to one, that the reporter of a miracle tells a lie.

THOMAS PAINE

3. Did *The Passion of the Christ* conclude the way you expected? Explain your response. How similar do you think the film's ending is to the account given in the Bible?

4. What did you like or dislike about the film's portrayal of the resurrection? How did seeing Jesus alive again make you feel?

The resurrection showed that the crucifixion was no defeat, but part of God's plan . . . It was an act of God that vindicated Jesus' personal claims to divinity.

WILLIAM LANE CRAIG

5. What do you think was the significance of showing Jesus alive and well in the last scene of the movie?

6. Using the chart below, indicate to what degree of certainty you believe that the resurrection actually occurred. Explain your response.

1	2	3	4	5	6	7	8	9	10
I am very certain the resurrection never occurred.				I am unsure if the resurrection occurred.				I am very certain the resurrection occurred.	

7. Does it matter that Jesus rose from the dead? Why or why not? If Jesus' death was not final, what impact does that have on you?

8. Read the Bible verses below. What purpose do you think Jesus' resurrection achieved? What does the resurrection say about Jesus' ability to conquer death? Forgive sins?

> "Men of Israel, listen to this: Jesus of Nazareth was a man accredited by God to you by miracles, wonders and signs, which God did among you through him, as you yourselves know. This man was handed over to you by God's set purpose and foreknowledge; and you, with the help of wicked men, put him to death by nailing him to the cross. But God raised him from the dead, freeing him from the agony of death, because it was impossible for death to keep its hold on him."
>
> Acts 2:22–24

> For Christ died for sins once for all, the righteous for the unrighteous, to bring you to God. He was put to death in the body but made alive by the Spirit.
>
> 1 Peter 3:18

> "Do not be afraid. I am the First and the Last. I am the Living One; I was dead, and behold I am alive for ever and ever! And I hold the keys of death and Hades."
>
> Revelation 1:17–18

The earliest Christians didn't just endorse Jesus' teachings; they were convinced they had seen him alive after the crucifixion. *That's* what changed their lives and started the church. Certainly, since this was their centermost conviction, they would have made absolutely sure that it was true.

GARY HABERMAS

9. Do you agree with the following Bible verses, that the Christian faith hinges on the resurrection? Why or why not?

And if Christ has not been raised, our preaching is useless and so is your faith. More than that, we are then found to be false witnesses about God, for we have testified about God that he raised Christ from the dead ... And if Christ has not been raised, your faith is futile; you are still in your sins. Then those also who have fallen asleep in Christ are lost. If only for this life we have hope in Christ, we are to be pitied more than all men.

1 Corinthians 15:14–19

The Resurrection of Debbie

Gary Habermas is a university professor who is considered one of the world's leading authorities on the resurrection. For him, a very personal experience illustrated the relevance of Christ's passion for today.

In 1995, his wife, Debbie, was slowly dying of stomach cancer. "This was the worst thing that could possibly happen," said Habermas. "But do you know what was amazing? My students would call me—not just one, but several of them—and say, 'At a time like this, aren't you glad about the resurrection?' As sober as these circumstances were, I had to smile for two reasons. First, my students were trying to cheer me up with my own teaching. And second, it worked.

"As I would sit there, I'd picture Job, who went through all that terrible stuff and asked questions of

God, but then God turned the tables and asked *him* a few questions. I knew if God were to come to me, I'd ask only one question: 'Lord, why is Debbie up there in bed?' And I think God would respond by asking gently, 'Gary, did I raise my son from the dead?' I'd say, 'Come on, Lord, I've written seven books on that topic! Of course he was raised from the dead. But I want to know about Debbie!'

"I think he'd keep coming back to the same question 'Did I raise my son from the dead?' 'Did I raise my son from the dead?' until I got his point. The resurrection says that if Jesus was raised two thousand years ago, there's an answer to Debbie's death in 1995. And do you know what? It worked for me [then], and it still works today.

"Losing my wife was the most painful experience I've ever had to face, but if the resurrection could get me through that, it can get me through anything. It was good for AD 30, it's good for 1995, it's good for 1998, and it's good beyond that.

"That's not some sermon. I believe that with all my heart. If there's a resurrection, there's a heaven. If Jesus was raised, Debbie will be raised. And I will be someday too.

"Then I'll see them both."

I say unequivocally that the evidence for the resurrection of Jesus Christ is so overwhelming that it compels acceptance by proof which leaves absolutely no room for doubt.

SIR LIONEL LUCKHOO

---

10. What hope does Jesus' resurrection give you that life after death is possible? What other implications does the resurrection have for you? For example, how would your view of life, death, and the afterlife change if the resurrection has or has not occurred?

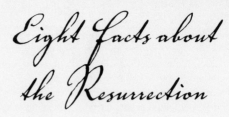

Eight Facts about the Resurrection

Jesus' empty grave is reported in extremely early sources that date so close to the event that they could not have been products of legend.

The fact that the gospels report women discovered the empty tomb bolsters their credibility. In a culture where women were considered unreliable witnesses, surely the writers would have claimed men found the tomb vacant if they were fabricating the story.

The site of Jesus' tomb was known to both Christians and their opponents, so it could have been checked by skeptics.

Nobody—not even Roman or Jewish leaders—ever claimed the tomb still contained Jesus' body. Instead, they claimed the disciples, despite having no motive or opportunity, had stolen the body—an outlandish theory critics have long since abandoned.

The evidence for Jesus' numerous post-resurrection appearances didn't develop gradually over the years as mythology distorted memories of his life. Rather, the resurrection was the church's central proclamation from the beginning.

According to psychologist Gary Collins, the appearances of Jesus cannot be attributed to hallucinations or wishful thinking.

Apart from the resurrection, there's no reasonable explanation for why skeptics like Paul and James would have been converted and died for their new-found faith.

The miraculous emergence of the church in the very city where the crucifixion took place is inexplicable apart from eyewitnesses telling the truth about seeing Jesus alive again.

Concludes British theologian Michael Green: "The appearances of Jesus are as well authenticated as anything in antiquity . . . There can be no rational doubt that they occurred."

> I know pretty well what evidence is, and I tell you, such evidence as that for the resurrection has never broken down yet.
>
> JOHN SINGLETON COPLEY

11. Read 1 Corinthians 15:3–7 below. How is your belief or disbelief in the resurrection influenced by this very early biblical testimony of the many witnesses who saw Jesus alive after the crucifixion?

> For what I received I passed on to you as of first importance: that Christ died for our sins according to the Scriptures, that he was buried, that he was raised on the third day according to the Scriptures, and that he appeared to Peter, and then to the Twelve. After that, he appeared to more than five hundred of the brothers at the same time, most of whom are still living, though some have fallen asleep. Then he appeared to James, then to all the apostles.
>
> 1 Corinthians 15:3–7

But God raised him from the dead, freeing him from the agony of death, because it was impossible for death to keep its hold on him.

ACTS 2:24

12. Jesus said, "I am the resurrection and the life. He who believes in me will live, even though he dies; and whoever lives and believes in me will never die. Do you believe this?" (John 11:25–26). Explain what you think Jesus means. Do you believe him? Why or why not?

13. Check the statement(s) below that best describes your position at this point. Share your selection with the rest of the group and give reasons for your response.

_____ I don't believe that the resurrection actually occurred.

_____ I think the resurrection is wishful thinking and no more.

_____ I believe the resurrection proves Jesus has the power to defeat death and forgive sins.

_____ I believe the resurrection occurred, but I'm not sure what that means to me.

_____ I'll need more evidence before I'll believe in the resurrection.

_____ I wish I could accept the resurrection as fact, but I'm just not there yet.

_____ Write your own phrase here: _____
_____
_____

> Without the resurrection, our faith is dead; the story's incomplete without it.
>
> MEL GIBSON

Scripture for Further Study

- Matthew 27:39–66
- John 10:17–18
- John 11:25–17
- Romans 14:9
- 1 Corinthians 15:1–58
- 1 Thessalonians 4:13–14

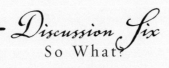

Discussion Six
So What?

HOW IS THIS STORY RELEVANT TO ME?

"Tell me another story!"

We begged for stories when we were children. We couldn't wait to crawl into bed and hear our favorite fairy tale. Stories helped us cope with fears or escape from reality into our dreams. They captivated us with thrilling characters, dramatic conflict, dangerous missions, and narrow escapes. Stories were a safe introduction to the big, wide world. Through them, we understood a little bit about good and evil, adventure, and heroic deeds.

Even as we become adults, stories still enlighten us about the world around us. They still teach us about good and evil. They reveal profound insights about human nature or remind us not to take ourselves too seriously. They give us themes to cheer about and causes to root for. It seems every good story offers something about life and love. Something about truth.

These days film has taken the art of storytelling to a whole new level. Through technology we can watch dramas unfold on an enormous screen, complete with musical scores, special effects, and digital sound. Like the tales from childhood, these productions make lasting impressions.

We watch film after film and laugh about a slapstick scene, quote a memorable line, or ponder a thoughtful premise. Then every once in a while we stumble on a truly inspirational story—one so

63

moving, so gripping, that it transforms us. That's what we've been looking for our whole lives. We long for the story that seizes us at the core of our soul.

Two great storytellers talked about this very thing one dark night in England a few decades ago, as biographer Humphrey Carpenter recounts.

"Just as a *word* is an invention about an object or an idea," said J. R. R. Tolkien as they walked the grounds of Magdalen College, "so a *story* can be an invention about *Truth*."

"I've loved stories since I was a boy," responded C. S. "Jack" Lewis. "You know that! Especially stories about heroism and sacrifice, death and resurrection . . . But when it comes to Christianity, well, that's another matter. I simply don't understand how the life and death of Someone Else (whoever he was) two thousand years ago can help *me* here and now."

"But don't you see, Jack?" persisted Tolkien. "The Christian story is the greatest story of them all. Because it's the *Real Story*. The *historical event* that fulfills the tales and shows us what they mean . . . not just a verbal invention."

Lewis turned. "Are you trying to tell me that in the story of Christ all the other stories have somehow *come true?*"

Ten days later, Lewis wrote a letter to another friend: "I have just passed on from believing in God to definitely believing in Christ—in Christianity. My long night talk with Tolkien had a great deal to do with it."

The Passion of the Christ is the moving film version of the very same story that Tolkien and Lewis discussed all those years ago. Tolkien claimed it is The Story that satisfies all stories. It's the one powerful, historical event that fulfills all our deepest hopes and longings. It gripped Tolkien's soul. It revolutionized Lewis's life. It has transformed countless others throughout history. And it continues to impact people today.

Maybe it's the story that *you've* been looking for your whole life.

Christianity is a statement which, if false, is of *no* importance, and, if true, of infinite importance. The one thing it cannot be is moderately important.

C. S. LEWIS

Open for Discussion ―――――

1. What stories have you heard as a child or as an adult that have made a significant difference in your life? What impact did they have on you?

2. How has viewing *The Passion of the Christ* changed you? In what ways do you feel drawn to respond to this film?

> My hope is that anyone who goes in and can manage to stay through [*The Passion of the Christ*] and suffer through with it—that they're changed when they leave. I hope the viewers come out of the movie theater with a lot of questions.
>
> MEL GIBSON

3. According to the verse below, Christ died and rose again to make payment for sins. How would you define sin? What are the repercussions of sin, if any?

    For Christ died for sins once for all, the righteous for the unrighteous, to bring you to God. He was put to death in the body but made alive by the Spirit.

    1 Peter 3:18

4. Read the verses below. Do you agree or disagree with the biblical teaching that we have all sinned against God and, therefore, we all need his forgiveness through Christ? Which statements do you agree or disagree with?

You see, at just the right time, when we were still powerless, Christ died for the ungodly. Very rarely will anyone die for a righteous man, though for a good man someone might possibly dare to die. But God demonstrates his own love for us in this: While we were still sinners, Christ died for us.

Romans 5:6–8

All have sinned and fall short of the glory of God, and are justified freely by his grace through the redemption that came by Christ Jesus.

Romans 3:23

God made him who had no sin to be sin for us, so that in him we might become the righteousness of God.

2 Corinthians 5:21

God is just, holy, and morally perfect. We all stand guilty before God because we fall far short of his perfection. But the Bible also reveals that God is loving and merciful. He has provided a way to escape the condemnation we deserve. He has sent his Son to die for us.

CLIFFE KNECHTLE

5. According to the verses listed above, what is God's provision for solving the sin problem of the human race? How do you respond to this claim?

Our Spiritual Disease

When a person is diagnosed with an illness, taking certain medications may help ease the symptoms but do nothing to cure the actual disease. Other treatments may cure the disease itself and, as a result, the symptoms eventually disappear as well. The Bible teaches that the wrongs we commit on a daily basis are really signs or symptoms of a much deeper disease of the human heart: sin. Performing good works or being a good person is actually just a temporary treatment of the symptoms of our spiritual disease. Jesus Christ, who is God incarnate, provides the only complete and final cure by forgiving our sin and transforming our hearts.

6. Read the verses listed below. What is your reaction to the Bible's claims that it is absolutely impossible to do anything to save yourself from the penalty of sin? How difficult is it for you to admit that you cannot, on your own, bridge the gap between you and God caused by your sin?

For the wages of sin is death, but the gift of God is eternal life in Christ Jesus our Lord.

Romans 6:23

For it is by grace you have been saved, through faith—and this not from yourselves, it is the gift of God—not by works, so that no one can boast.

Ephesians 2:8–9

But when the kindness and love of God our Savior appeared, he saved us, not because of righteous things we had done, but because of his mercy. He saved us through the washing of rebirth and renewal by the Holy Spirit, whom he poured out on us generously through Jesus Christ

our Savior, so that, having been justified by his grace, we might become heirs having the hope of eternal life.

Titus 3:4–7

"For God so loved the world that he gave his one and only Son, that whoever believes in him shall not perish but have eternal life. For God did not send his Son into the world to condemn the world, but to save the world through him. Whoever believes in him is not condemned, but whoever does not believe stands condemned already because he has not believed in the name of God's one and only Son."

John 3:16–18

God made [Jesus] who had no sin to be sin for us, so that in him we might become the righteousness of God.

2 Corinthians 5:21

7. What is it about Jesus that, according to the Bible, enabled him to become the only worthy payment for sin and therefore the only possible bridge between God and all of humanity?

8. Acts 4:12 says, "Salvation is found in no one else, for there is no other name under heaven given to men by which we must be saved."

What reasons do you think the Bible gives for its assertion that Jesus is the only way to God?

9. Read Philippians 2:6–11 below. What difference does it make to you, if any, that Jesus Christ came into the world, lived a perfect life, died on the cross for your sins, and rose again?

   [Jesus], being in very nature God, did not consider equality with God something to be grasped, but made himself nothing, taking the very nature of a servant, being made in human likeness. And being found in appearance as a man, he humbled himself and became obedient to death—even death on a cross! Therefore God exalted him to the highest place and gave him the name that is above every name, that at the name of Jesus every knee should bow, in heaven and on earth and under the earth, and every tongue confess that Jesus Christ is Lord, to the glory of God the Father.

   Philippians 2:6–11

10. The following verses describe an encounter Thomas had with Jesus soon after the resurrection. How do you identify with Thomas's doubts? How challenging is it for you to believe in Jesus without seeing him?

    Now Thomas, one of the Twelve, was not with the disciples when Jesus came. So the other disciples told him, "We have seen the Lord!"

But he said to them, "Unless I see the nail marks in his hands and put my finger where the nails were, and put my hand into his side, I will not believe it."

A week later his disciples were in the house again, and Thomas was with them. Though the doors were locked, Jesus came and stood among them and said, "Peace be with you!" Then he said to Thomas, "Put your finger here; see my hands. Reach out your hand and put it into my side. Stop doubting and believe."

Thomas said to him, "My Lord and my God!"

Then Jesus told him, "Because you have seen me, you have believed; blessed are those who have not seen and yet have believed."

Jesus did many other miraculous signs in the presence of his disciples, which are not recorded in this book. But these are written that you may believe that Jesus is the Christ, the Son of God, and that by believing you may have life in his name.

John 20:24–31

11. Romans 10:9 says, "If you confess with your mouth, 'Jesus is Lord,' and believe in your heart that God raised him from the dead, you will be saved." Does anything keep you from declaring the resurrected Jesus as the forgiver of your sins and leader of your life? If you're comfortable doing so, tell the group where you are with this decision. If there is anything holding you back, share that as well.

Jump in the Wheelbarrow

Intellectual assent to Christianity means to acknowledge, as a piece of information, that Jesus came into the world to save sinners. Personal acceptance is trusting that information enough to apply it to your own life. Years ago, the great acrobat Karl Wallenda stretched a wire across Niagara Falls and offered to carry anyone across in a wheelbarrow. There were many who "believed" he could do it, but no takers. To actually get in the wheelbarrow and be taken across the chasm—*that's* the difference between intellectual assent and personal acceptance.

12. In John 5:24, Jesus says, "I tell you the truth, whoever hears my word and believes him who sent me has eternal life and will not be condemned; he has crossed over from death to life." And John 1:12 says, "Yet to all who received him, to those who believed in his name, he gave the right to become children of God." According to these verses, what do we need to do to be assured of eternal life? What does God do?

13. Jesus described the essence of eternal life when he said, "This is eternal life: that they may know you, the only true God, and Jesus Christ, whom you have sent" (John 17:3). The phrase "to know" can also mean "to share intimately." What light does this shed on the true meaning of eternal life and on God's intention for our relationship with him?

And this is the testimony: God has given us eternal life, and this life is in his Son. He who has the Son has life; he who does not have the Son of God does not have life.

1 JOHN 5:11–12

14. The epilogue to this guide recounts an incident that involved one of the authors. Read the story on page 75 and discuss your reaction to it. What factors will determine how you might respond to the choice that is described?

15 Now that we're at the end of this discussion guide, how would you characterize where you are in your spiritual journey? Check the statement(s) below that best describes your position at this point. Share your selection with the rest of the group and give reasons for your response.

_____ I'm still not certain what relevance Jesus has for me today.

_____ If God really cares for me the way the Bible claims he does, then I still don't understand why Jesus is necessary to bring us together.

_____ I have a difficult time believing that all I have to do is accept Jesus to receive God's forgiveness.

_____ I'd like to learn more about what it really means to have a relationship with God.

_____ I am glad to finally understand what being a Christian means.

_____ I now have a better grasp of how the Bible would say some people are Christians and others aren't, but I don't agree.

_____ I am grateful that God has provided a way for me to be reconciled to him.

_____ I understand that Jesus is the only way to get to God, but I'm not sure how I feel about it.

_____ I understand that the only way to have a relationship with God is through Jesus; however, I am either unwilling or not ready to take that step.

_____ I understand the need for Jesus, since he is the only way I can be forgiven, be reconciled to God, and receive eternal life, so I want to take that step.

_____ Write your own phrase here: _____
_____
_____

Scripture for Further Study

- Isaiah 59:2
- John 1:10-12
- John 6:35-40
- John 17:3
- Romans 6:23
- Ephesians 1:7-8

- Ephesians 2:1-10
- Titus 3:4-7
- 1 Peter 1:18-21
- Hebrews 1:1-3
- Hebrews 12:1-4
- 1 John 1:8-9

Only the Beginning

And for us this is the end of all the stories, and we can most truly say that they all lived happily ever after. But for them it was only the beginning of the real story. All their life in this world and all their adventures in Narnia had only been the cover and the title page: now at last they were beginning Chapter One of the Great Story which no one on earth has read: which goes on for ever: in which every chapter is better than the one before.

C. S. LEWIS

THE PAYMENT AND THE CHOICE

An acquaintance called with what he said was an embarrassing request: His little girl had been caught shoplifting from our church bookstore, and he wanted to know if I (Lee) would represent the church so she could come and apologize. He said he wanted to use this incident as a teaching moment. I agreed—but I had a much bigger lesson in mind.

The next day, the parents and their eight-year-old daughter trooped into my office and sat down. "Tell me what happened," I said to the little girl as gently as I could.

"Well," she said as she started to sniffle, "I saw a book that I really wanted, but I didn't have any money . . ." Now tears formed in her eyes and spilled down her cheeks. I handed her a tissue. "So I put the book under my coat and took it. I knew it was wrong. I knew I shouldn't do it, but I did. And I'm sorry. I'll never do it again. Honest!"

"I'm so glad you're willing to admit what you did and say you're sorry," I told her. "That's very brave, and it's the right thing to do. But what do you think an appropriate punishment would be?"

She shrugged. I thought for a moment before saying, "I understand the book cost five dollars. I think it would be fair if you paid the bookstore five dollars,

plus three times that amount, which would make the total twenty dollars. Do you think that would be fair?"

She nodded sadly. "Yes," she murmured. She could see the fairness in that. But now there was fear in her eyes. Twenty dollars is a mountain of money for a little kid. Where would she ever come up with that much cash?

I wanted to use this moment to teach her something about Jesus. So I opened my desk drawer, removed my checkbook, and wrote out a check on my personal account for the full amount. I tore off the check and held it out to her. Her mouth dropped open.

"I'm going to pay your penalty so you don't have to. Do you know why I'd do that?" Bewildered, she shook her head. "Because I love you. Because I care about you. Because you're valuable to me. And please remember this: that's how Jesus feels about you too. *Except even more.*"

At that moment, she reached out and accepted my gift. I wish I could find the words to describe the look of absolute relief and joy and wonder that blossomed on her face. She was almost giddy with gratitude!

And that's a little bit like what Jesus is offering to do for you. By his suffering and death on the cross, he paid the penalty for your wrongdoing, as your substitute, so you wouldn't have to. Out of his love for you, he's offering that payment as a pure gift—which you're free to accept or reject. Saying yes to him is as easy as a prayer in which you turn from your sin, ask for God's forgiveness and leadership of your life, and receive his promise of heaven.

It's your choice.

Here is a trustworthy saying that deserves full acceptance: Christ Jesus came into the world to save sinners.

1 TIMOTHY 1:15

Recommended Resources
for Further Investigation

The Case for Christ by Lee Strobel (Zondervan)

The Case for Easter by Lee Strobel (Zondervan)

The Case for Faith by Lee Strobel (Zondervan)

Give Me an Answer by Cliffe Knechtle (InterVarsity)

God's Outrageous Claims by Lee Strobel (Zondervan)

The Historical Jesus by Gary Habermas (College Press)

I Don't Have Enough Faith to be an Atheist by Norman Geisler and Frank Turek (Crossway)

Jesus Among Other Gods by Ravi Zacharias (Word)

Jesus Under Fire edited by J. P. Moreland and Michael J. Wilkins (Zondervan)

Know What You Believe by Paul Little (InterVarsity)

Know Why You Believe by Paul Little (InterVarsity)

Mere Christianity by C. S. Lewis (Harper San Francisco)

More Than A Carpenter by Josh McDowell (Here's Life)

The New Testament Documents: Are They Reliable? by F. F. Bruce (Eerdmans)

The Purpose-Driven Life by Rick Warren (Zondervan)

The Reality Check Series by Mark Ashton (Zondervan)

The Risen Jesus and Future Hope by Gary Habermas (Rowman and Littlefield)

The Tough Questions Series by Garry Poole and Judson Poling (Zondervan)

Who Made God? edited by Ravi Zacharias and Norman Geisler (Zondervan)

Acknowledgments

This guide was the product of teamwork—not just between the authors, but also involving a host of others who contributed in a variety of ways.

Special thanks goes to Ann Kroeker, Laura Allen, and Jim Poole for their creative insights, ideas, and suggestions. Their outstanding contributions in the area of writing and editing helped take this guide to the next level.

The team at Zondervan—including Scott Bolinder, Lyn Cryderman, John Topliff, Jack Kuhatschek, John Raymond, Angela Scheff, Bob Hudson, Cindy Davis, Todd Sprague, and others—was terrific in producing this resource in record time. We also want to express our appreciation to Scott Evans and Doug Martinez of Outreach, Inc., and the Willow Creek Association.

Finally, we're grateful for the vision and courage that prompted Mel Gibson to produce a motion picture that finally portrays the passion of Jesus with unflinching realism.

LEE STROBEL

Former atheist Lee Strobel, educated at Yale Law School, was the award-winning legal editor of the *Chicago Tribune*. He has been a teaching pastor at two of America's largest churches and has written or coauthored a dozen books, including the bestsellers *The Case for Christ* and *The Case for Faith*. His latest books are *The Case for a Creator* and *The Case for Easter*. He and his wife, Leslie, live in Southern California.

GARRY POOLE

Garry Poole is the director of evangelism at Willow Creek Community Church in South Barrington, Illinois, where his responsibilities include overseeing a network of small groups designed to help spiritual seekers investigate Christianity. He is the author of *Seeker Small Groups* and *The Complete Book of Questions* and the coauthor of the bestselling Tough Questions series. He lives in suburban Chicago.